# SCOTLAND & ROME

## Centuries of Enrichment

ITALIAN CULTURAL INSTITUTE EDINBURGH
– 2010 –

Published to accompany an exhibition held at the
Royal Scottish Academy

13 September – 30 September 2010

SCOTTISH
CATHOLIC
ARCHIVES

We would like to thank Finmeccanica
for supporting this publication.

# CONTENTS

# FOREWORDS

## FIONA HYSLOP, MINSTER FOR CULTURE & EXTERNAL AFFAIRS, THE SCOTTISH GOVERNMENT

I very much welcome the Royal Scottish Academy exhibition, 'Scotland and Rome' which provides a fantastic opportunity to highlight and recognise the strong links between Scotland and Italy. I am especially pleased that the exhibition will provide the chance to view items that incorporate treasures from both Scotland's National Collections together with rare items from the Scottish Catholic Archives.

The Scottish Government is strongly committed to building closer relations with our European partners and seeks opportunities to work with our neighbours to share experience and learn from each other. This is a great example of partnership working between the Italian Cultural Institute, National Galleries of Scotland, National Library of Scotland and the Hunterian Museum together with support from the Archdiocese of Glasgow which has enabled pieces to be loaned from the Scottish Catholic Archives.

Scotland is a positive, welcoming and outward-looking member of the international community. In the 1800's many Italian families arrived to settle in Scotland, bringing with them their own culture and traditions. Over the years the relationship between our two cultures has developed and grown into something unique. We now have many successful Scots Italians in all walks of life from Peter Capaldi to Dario Franchitti and Sharleen Spiteri.

It therefore gives me great pleasure to lend my support to what is sure to be a very popular and timely exhibition, opening as it does, around the time of the visit by His Holiness Pope Benedict XVI to Scotland in September 2010.

I hope that you take the time to enjoy the exhibition.

Very best wishes

**Fiona Hyslop**
***Minister for Culture and External Affairs***
***The Scottish Government***

## H.E. ALAIN GIORGIO MARIA ECONOMIDES, ITALIAN AMBASSADOR TO THE UNITED KINGDOM

It is impossible to speak of western civilisation without talking of Rome, not so much on account of her former role as an imperial, conquering power, but rather because of the immense cultural, artistic and lawmaking legacy she has left us. It might seem at first sight that Scotland was one of the peripheral areas least marked by Roman civilisation, but a closer look reveals profound and very close links.

This exhibition, *Scotland and Rome*, aims to highlight and provide evidence for at least some of the many continuing links between Rome and Scotland over the last two thousand years. All the exhibits come from Scottish collections.

Beginning with archaeological finds in Scotland, particularly from the Antonine Wall, held in the Hunterian Museum, it moves on to medieval evidence showing the close relationship between Scotland and the very centre of western Christianity, established in the city of Rome. Then it is the turn of the Renaissance and Baroque periods, with their interest in the rediscovered texts of classical literature, here represented by the priceless volumes from the National Library of Scotland and the Scottish Catholic Archives. That extraordinary phenomenon, the Grand Tour, shows that, for the élite at least, a visit to Rome was an essential part of a gentleman's education. This ideal itinerary is represented by paintings, drawings and prints, courtesy of the National Galleries of Scotland.

Present day connections are represented by the works of Scottish artists chosen by the Royal Scottish Academy, in whose Library the present exhibition is being held.

Our warmest, most heartfelt thanks go to all the organisations and individuals whose help has allowed us to make this journey through Scottish-Roman relations possible.

**HE Alain Giorgio Maria Economides**
***Italian Ambassador to the United Kingdom***

## MOST REVEREND MARIO CONTI, ARCHBISHOP OF GLASGOW, PRESIDENT, HERITAGE COMMISSION, BISHOPS' CONFERENCE OF SCOTLAND

I welcome this exhibition, *Scotland and Rome*, and its opportune timing, to coincide with the visit of the Bishop of Rome, His Holiness Pope Benedict XVI, to the United Kingdom. We in Scotland will have the privilege of welcoming him first.

The Italian Ambassador to the Court of St James's has underlined the immense influence of Rome on the development of Western civilisation. Everywhere in Scotland we gather evidence of this: whether with our physical eye alighting on Edinburgh's New Town, or with the eye of the legal eagle on Scots law, with the ear tuned to early Scots Renaissance music or with the imagination of the engineer focused on the construction of some of our finest buildings.

The Pope arrives providentially on the Feast of St Ninian, according to tradition educated in Rome and our first named missionary of the Christian faith in Scotland. The signature of Rome, *SPQR* – *Senatus Populusque Romanus*, gave way to the chi-rho – the monogram of Christ, or the *labarum* by which Constantine prevailed, as some of our earliest Christian monuments show.

Indeed, for a thousand years, Rome virtually belonged to the Popes, and only ceased to be a papal city in 1870 at the time of the *Risorgimento*.

We would overlook the obvious if we failed to recognise that so much of Roman culture was insinuated in the development of Scotland, even after the Reformation, by those who were trained in its systems as Heralds of the Gospel. And if its ancient and beautiful language is still heard, it is likely to be in the liturgy of the Church.

Scotland's sons, whether in the arts or in the Church, made their own contributions to that cultural pot, be they painters such as Gavin Hamilton, antiquarians such as James Byres, or churchmen as the Abbé Paul MacPherson, who, in recompense for his services to the Holy See and to Scotland at the time of the Napoleonic invasion, was given a most beautiful chalice inscribed by Pope Leo XII, for the Church of Glenlivet!

I hope that all who visit this Exhibition will be stimulated to remember things they already know and learn new things to enrich their memories.

**Most Rev. Mario Conti, Archbishop of Glasgow**
***President, Heritage Commission, Bishops' Conference of Scotland***

FORTVNAE
VEXILLA
TIONES
LEG II AVG
LEG VI VIC

# SCOTLAND & THE ROMANS

PROFESSOR DAVID J. BREEZE

Scotland always lay on the edge of the Roman world, but it was not *terra incognita*. Even before the Roman army ventured into northern Scotland by land or the Roman fleet sailed round its northern coasts in the early AD 80s, something was known of its geography. For example, the existence of the three archipelagos, Orkney, Shetland and the Outer Hebrides, was recorded. Indeed, nearly 400 years before the first Roman invasion, Pytheas of Marseilles explored these northern seas, reporting that land was known even beyond Scotland.

Rome's relationship with northern Britain was essentially military. For most of the period during which Britain was part of the Roman Empire, that is from AD 43 to 410, the northern frontier of the province lay on Hadrian's Wall, though advance forts lay further north. On several occasions Roman armies marched north from this line, thrice occupying southern Scotland. The first occupation was initiated by the invasion of the governor Julius Agricola in 79. Agricola campaigned north of the Tay and defeated the Caledonians in battle at Mons Graupius, the location of which is unknown. Disasters elsewhere, however, led to the abandonment of his conquests shortly afterwards. This period of occupation lasted no more than ten years

Left: **Altar to Fortuna** Hunterian Museum, University of Glasgow

The Roman army withdrew to the Tyne-Solway isthmus, roughly from Newcastle to Carlisle, and it was here that Hadrian's Wall was erected in the 120s. The death of the Emperor Hadrian in 138 resulted in a significant change. His frontier was abandoned and his successor, Antoninus Pius, ordered an advance to the Forth-Clyde isthmus, roughly from Bo'ness to Old Kilpatrick, where a new wall – the Antonine Wall – was built. This occupation lasted about twenty years before the army withdrew to Hadrian's Wall, which was re-commissioned.

The final invasion and occupation of southern Scotland came another forty years later. In 208, the Emperor Septimius Severus came to Britain with the intention of solving the problem of the northern frontier by conquering the rest of the island. Although he met with some success, his venture ended with his death at York in 211 and the abandonment of the newly conquered territory when his sons returned to Rome.

Roman sources indicate that there were other occasions when the Romans and their northern neighbours clashed. Nor did the Romans always have it their own way. In 180 a Roman general was killed and in 197 peace with the Caledonians had to be bought by the Romans, who received in return some prisoners-of-war. In the early 4th century, the situation was so serious that the emperor himself led the campaign against the Picts.

These activities have left in Scotland one of the greatest legacies of Roman military remains to be found anywhere in the Roman Empire. They include the earthworks of camps, forts, towers, roads – and the north-west frontier of the Roman Empire, the Antonine Wall. This stretched across central Scotland from the Forth to the Clyde, consisting of a turf rampart on a stone base fronted by a wide and deep ditch. Along its line lay forts connected by a road. It was erected by the three legions of Britain. These left records of their work in a series of inscriptions known as distance slabs (so called because they record the distance constructed by each legion). They are very specific, calculating the measurements to less than a pace. Several of these records are accompanied by scenes of fighting and victory, depicting the support of the gods for Roman endeavours. They are unique in the Roman Empire and probably relate to the reason for the invasion of the 140s.

Antoninus Pius was not Hadrian's first choice of successor and he came to the throne with no military experience, both facts well known to the Roman aristocracy. Antoninus may therefore have decided that a short, successful war would provide him with military prestige, so important for a Roman emperor.

This was triumphantly achieved and it seems likely that the purpose of the distance slabs was to remind everyone of the gods' support for the new emperor.

There are many other artefacts in Scotland's museums which reflect contact between Rome and her northern neighbours. Roman objects have been found as for north as Shetland and as far west at the Outer Hebrides. They indicate contact, perhaps trade or gifts from Roman officers to local chiefs. Certainly one of the gifts which the modern world has received through the Roman Empire is Christianity. It is probable that Christian missionaries had reached southern Scotland before the end of Roman rule in Britain, and converted the local rulers. This was the start of a long relationship. The link between Rome and Christianity is reflected in an object found in many churches today: the banner. This is the lineal descendant of the Roman military flag. Its appearance in today's churches is because the Emperor Constantine ordered the Christian symbol to be placed on his military flags before the battle of the Milvan Bridge in 312. His success led to the triumph of Christianity – and the physical survival of the Roman flag.

**Distance Slab from the Antonine Wall (Not on Display)**
Hunterian Museum, University of Glasgow

**Bronze Double-chain Brooch**
Hunterian Museum, University of Glasgow

# ROMAN OBJECTS FROM NORTHERN BRITAIN

Louisa Hammersley, University of Glasgow

Although the Roman campaigns in Scotland were intermittent and the subsequent occupations short-lived, a rich collection of material has survived to demonstrate the significant impact that Rome had upon the existing inhabitants of the region immediately within and beyond the north-western frontier of Empire.

Since the initial acquisition by the University of Glasgow of an inscribed stone of the Twentieth Legion from the Marquis of Montrose during the 17th Century, the Roman collection at the Hunterian Museum has continued to expand to the extent that the museum now holds the pre-eminent collection of Roman artefacts in Scotland. In 1768 the University of Glasgow published a volume of these inscribed stones, *Monumenta Romani imperii...* , containing thirty engravings incorporating the name of the donor, year of acquisition (where known) and measurements of the original stone. The volume in this exhibition is held in Glasgow University Library Special Collections department.

Legionary stones, known as distance slabs, recovered from along the Antonine Wall, accurately record the length of wall completed by each legion. Of the nineteen known, seventeen are now in the Hunterian Museum. This body of material is unique, and nothing comparable has been found on any other frontier of the Roman Empire. The heavily-abbreviated Latin inscriptions are often accompanied by propagandist representations of Legionary emblems or scenes featuring fighting and victory, depicting the gods' support for the Roman campaigns and the militarily inexperienced new Emperor, Antoninus Pius. Other stones found along the Wall include tombstones and altars which give us important information about the people who manned, and interacted with, Roman forts.

One such altar in the collection was recovered from Castlecary fort, Falkirk, near the centre of the line of the Antonine Wall and is dedicated by the Second and Sixth Legions to Fortuna, the Roman goddess of good fortune. The altar is of the classic rectangular shape with a bowl-like feature carved into the top for the pouring of libations – liquid dedications – during prayers to the goddess. It has been engraved with the dedication:

> FORTVNAE VEXILLATIONES LEG II AVG LEG VI VIC
> P S P L L

which translates as:

> *To Fortune, detachments of the Second Augustan Legion (and) the Sixth Victorious Legion willingly and gladly set (this) up at their own expense*

The meaning of the final line (P S P L L) has never been satisfactorily explained and it is possible that this is a five-letter formulaic abbreviation.

The bath-house was a very important place for rest and recreation. Here military personnel took the opportunity to relax, to talk and play games. A half life-sized head of a goddess, included in the display, was recovered from the bath-house at Bearsden fort. This statue is unusual because it incorporates 'Celtic' features and is thought to have been a local representation of the goddess Fortuna, a favourite patron of bath-houses, or perhaps even a local deity. The fountainhead with a female head carved into the front was also recovered from the changing-room of Bearsden bathhouse, while the wall-mounted sandstone statuette, again of Fortuna, came from the interior of the bath-house at Castlecary. The pantheon of gods and goddesses was also commonly represented on portable objects that soldiers could carry with them on campaign, such as the bronze terminal with the head of the Minerva, the goddess of wisdom.

Other metalwork includes a complete copper-alloy jug from Sadlerhead, Lanarkshire, its handle exquisitely decorated with a female figure standing beside an altar or pedestal and holding a bird in her right hand. On the basis of typological parallels with another jug (recovered along with eleven bronze vessels from Rheinzabern, Germany) it is likely to be a 2nd-century import to Northern Britain. The final metal figure in the collection is a bronze head of a satyr, a free-spirited creature associated, in both Greek and Roman mythology, with woodland.

Roman family life is represented by a child's shoe which was recovered from a ditch at Bar Hill fort. This rare example of a leather sandal (*carbatina*) has elongated ankle loops and two shorter loops along each side, as well as stitch holes at the heel. It is an unusually well preserved and beautifully-crafted object, and may have belonged to a child of the fort's commanding officer, for the troops were not allowed to marry.

Metal craftsmanship was not restricted to the Roman army. Highly skilled local artisans produced the double-chained bronze brooch recovered from Leckie broch, Stirlingshire. The bronze chain measures 24cm and has brooches at each terminal, each a cast disc with loosely swivelling pin below, decorated with red and green enamel on the top surfaces. These skills are further displayed in another bronze brooch recovered from Leckie which comprises a disc with anchor-shaped ornamentation below, and a pin on the reverse; the brooch is also enamelled, this time with intricate brown and cream designs.

**Child's Leather Shoe (*carbatina*)**
Hunterian Museum, University of Glasgow

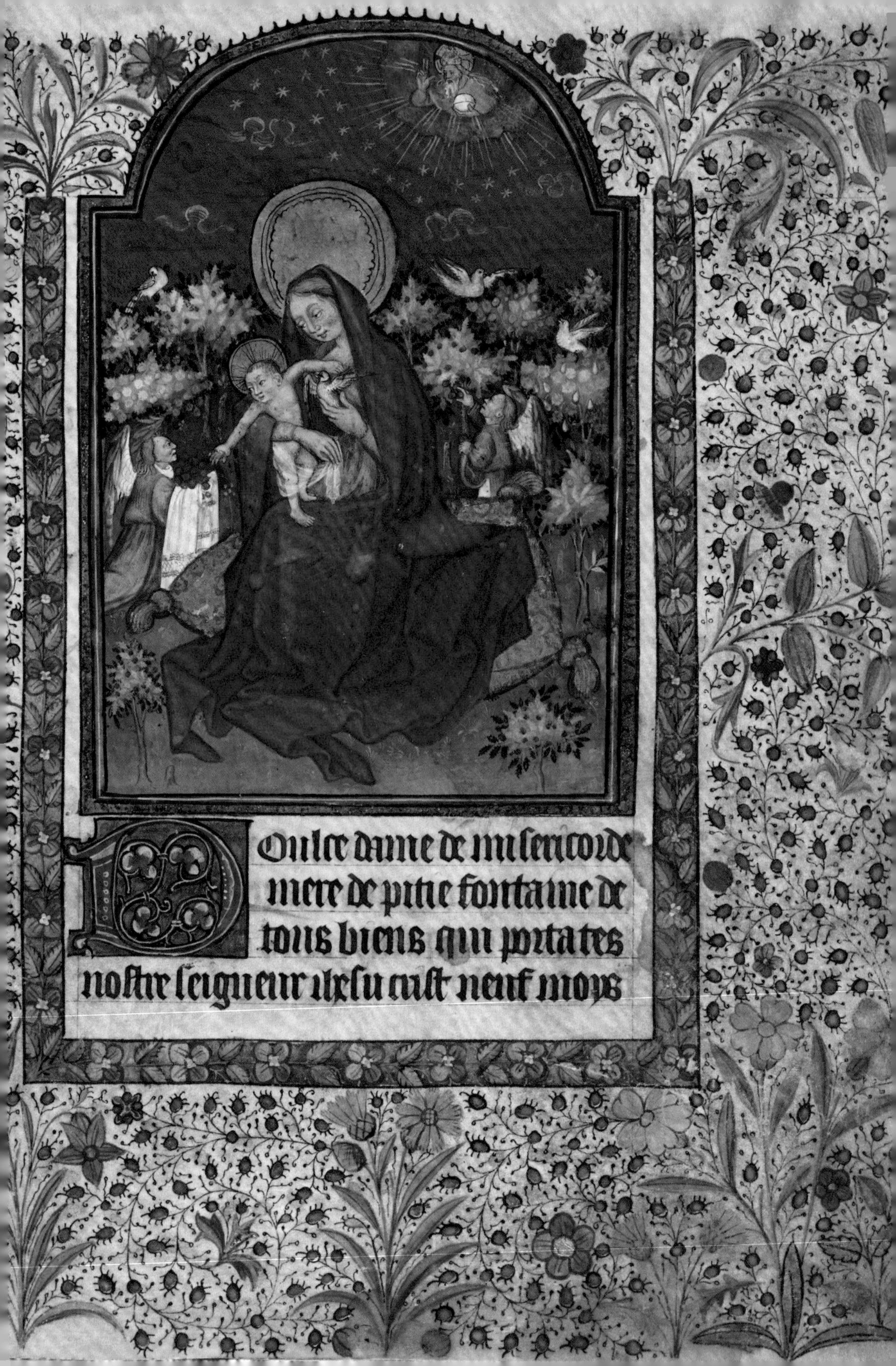

Doulce dame de misericorde
mere de pitie fontaine de
tous biens qui portates
nostre seigneur ihesu crist neuf moys

# SCOTLAND & THE HOLY SEE

## Dr Caroline Cradock, Scottish Catholic Archives

Christianity is believed to have been brought to Scotland by Saint Ninian in the 4th century, when he established Scotland's first church at Whithorn around the year 397. Of great influence also was St Columba who, around 563, set up a monastery on the island of Iona from whence a number of monks established houses throughout Scotland, Britain and the continent. In 1560 an Act of the Scottish Parliament established the Protestant faith in Scotland and made it a capital offence to celebrate Mass, to harbour priests or even to practice the Catholic religion. From then until the Catholic Relief Act of 1793, Catholics were persecuted to a greater or lesser extent, and Scotland became missionary territory.

The Jesuit mission to Scotland began in 1584. The hierarchy in Scotland had become extinct at the death of Archbishop James Beaton in 1603, and although there were always a few secular priests in Scotland, it was not until the appointment of William Ballantine as Prefect of the Mission in 1653 that they were reunited into a structured body. In 1695, Scotland gained its first Bishop since the Reformation with the appointment of Thomas Nicolson, a convert from Episcopalianism. His appointment was also significant in that it brought together, for the first time, the two missions of the secular priests and the Jesuits.

Left: **Hours of Marie de Rieux** 15th century
Scottish Catholic Archives

[illegible]

Þow mettist wiþ wõmẽ of levẽ
And also of Jerusalem
And alle wepte for þi torment
To hem þou seydist apertment
Ȝe wepe ȝe nouȝt for my wo
But for ȝour selfe & ȝour children also
For hem ȝe mowe wel sore wepe
And salte teres for hem lete
For þei schul haue turment hard
In hundrid wynt' afterward
Þo steppis of sine ȝeue vs pardon
Whan we go wiþ devocioun
In pilgrimage o hors or foot
Of alle our sinne þei be our boot

[illegible]

Þe nailes þoru feet & honden to
Þei kepe me out of sinne & wo
Þat I haue in my liue do
Wiþ hand handlid wiþ foot go

Malleus

Þe hamer þyþe sterne ī grete
Þat drof þe nailis þou hōd & fot
Þei be my socō þat in my liue
Oni mā smot wiþ staf or knyue

[illegible]

Þe vessel wiþ eysel & wiþ galle
Kepe me fro sinnes alle
Þat to þe soule is foul venim

And my vnbuxumnesse also
[illegible]

Ye laddre men vp set be crucifioun
When yow were ded to take ẏ doun
[illegible] I am lord in eny sinne
Saue me yat I drie nazt ẏ [illegible]
[illegible]

Ye tonge yat drow ye nail out
Of foot and hond al a bout
And losed his bodi fro ye tre
Of alle my sinnes yey losse me
[illegible]

Ye jew yat spit in yi face
For yow hit suffred zeue me grace
Yat I haue rewled or eni man me
For yat despit forzeue it me
[illegible]

Ye cros whiche he bar hys bak on
Yat he yolede dey vp on
Geue me grace in my liue
Of leue of sinne me to schriue
And ẏ to veray repentaunce
And tyme to fulfille my penaunce
[illegible]

Ye sepulcre yat in he was hid
His blessed bodi al for bled
[illegible] me sende or I dye
Sorwe of herte [illegible] yer in [illegible]
[illegible] clensid yat I be
Or I to my graue te
So yat I mowe at domesday
Go ye dome come wiy oute affray
And weend to blisse i companie
Yeras men schul neuer dye
But dwelle i Joye wt our lord [illegible]
Yer is day and neuer nizt
Yat laste schal wiy oute ende
Jhesu crist vs yiyer sende Amen
Thanke
Thanke ye lord yat you me wrozt
Your strong peinis ẏ me bout
Thank ye lord wiy rueful entent
Of yi peinis and yi turment
Wiy careful herte and drery mood
For schedyng of yi herte blood
What may I lord say to ye
Yi bodi was bounde to a tre
Wiy scourgis yer on smottis grete
Yi blessid bodi was forbete
In eche side turnid [illegible]
Also nakid so you were born
Yat [illegible] stede was founde non
So yi crowne to yi ton
Yi blessid bodi yer hit stood
Al hit was hid in yi blood
And when you were so forswonge
Among yeues yei ye hunge
Wiy scharpe nailis you hond ẏ feet
Yer ẏ henge til you were deed

[illegible]
Ye wikkid iewis wiy [illegible] mod
Lete yer out renne yi herte blod
Alas yi bodi was blac and blo
Our sinnes hit made so [illegible]
Yise instrumentis ben peintid here
In memorie of yi bitter [illegible]
Yer wiy yei duide yi passioun
Yei help vs to our sauacioun
For yei greued ye ful sore
I anguiis was euer [illegible] ẏ more
Lord what may I yer forzelde ye
You ne desirist but ẏ loue of me
Jhesu ye lord gif me grace and myzt
Wiy al my herte to loue ye rizt
In lijf in dey in wele and wo
Let neuer my herte turne ye fro
But mercy lord I ye pray
You lete me neuer in sinne day
[illegible] yat I may dampnid be
[illegible] ye lord for yi pite Amen

Yese armis of crist boye god and man
Seint petir ye pope descriued hem
What man yise armis ouersieth
You here sinnes [illegible]
[illegible] zer of pardoun is ye summe
Of seint petrus graunt pope of rome
And xxx papis aftur him yat war
ii.c. dayes eche zaf wiy good [illegible]
[illegible] bischopes eek also
[illegible] graunted bisides xl dayes ẏ to
Pope innocent made a gret counsail
And al yis confermed wt out fail
And more pardoun zaf al so
Four zer and xl dayes yer to
And eche pope i [illegible] to forward
For loue of ye vernicle he grant
l dayes to pardoun
And yer wiy al her [illegible]
And also to yat euer may
Yese armis of crist behold eu day
Wiy a good deuocioun
Yenkynge on cristes passioun
Yat day he get no wikkid ded
He be acumbred wiy no qued
And also to wommen hit is [illegible]
When yei schul trauaile of childe
Ye summe of alle to se hit eche day
ii.c. [illegible] zer and a half get man
Go se hit eche day ye mowe also
Fiue [illegible] zer [illegible] ẏ to
Go se hit [illegible] eche day eftir
[illegible] and ouzer
And half zer and dayes yere
Of pardon yese popes zeue yer
[illegible]

Details from
**Arma Christi (Instruments of Passion)**
15th-century roll of images and verses
Scottish Catholic Archives

An important document in the Scottish Catholic Archives, the *Visitation* by Alexander Leslie, gives our best insight into the state of the Catholic religion in Scotland towards the end of the 17th century. Leslie was a secular priest who visited almost all parts of the country in which Catholics were resident during the years 1677 and 1678. In 1681 he sent a report to the *Congregatione de Propaganda Fide* stating that there were 12,000 communicants in the Highlands and Islands, and 2,150 in the Lowlands.

The next century was a turbulent time for Scottish Catholics. While the reign of the Catholic monarch James VII improved things temporarily, his flight from Britain in 1688 was followed by anti-Catholic riots and destruction, and the Revolution of 1690 saw the imprisonment of fourteen secular priests.

Between 1727 and 1827 Scotland was divided into two vicariates: the Lowland and Highland Districts. Catholics more than ever were believed to be a subversive element and a danger to the Protestant State, and their association with Jacobitism severely damaged their standing in the community.

When England received the first Relief Bill in 1778 (removing some of the disadvantages Catholics had suffered), the intention had been to introduce it north of the border soon afterwards; but in Scotland in 1779 the mob were burning down and destroying the new Catholic chapel and house in Leith Wynd, Edinburgh. Much work was needed to turn public opinion around, and this is what Bishop John Geddes, who came to live in Edinburgh in 1781, began to do. He encouraged good relations with Protestants; urged his flock to play their part in the local community; and collected funds for the local hospital. At its second attempt, in 1793, the Catholic Relief Act in Scotland passed almost unopposed. By the end of this period, in 1827, there were thirty-one Catholic churches and twenty elementary schools in Scotland. Two years later, in 1829, a new seminary was opened: St Mary's College, Blairs, Aberdeenshire, after the great Catholic benefactor, Menzies of Pitfodels, left his house and estate to the Church for the purposes of the education of priests. Another Catholic Relief Act was passed in 1829, and this is generally perceived as the culmination of Catholic emancipation in the United Kingdom.

Between 1827 and 1878 Scotland was divided into three vicariates: the Eastern, the Western and the Northern. During the 19th century, Scotland's Catholic community experienced both significant immigration and emigration. Around the turn of the 19th-20th century it saw the emigration of large numbers of Highlanders to Canada and Australia, mainly due to crofting policies in Scotland.

PAVLVS EP·VS
Servus Servorum Dei

ad perpetuam
rei memoriam.

Omnis martyrii vis ac momentum, in quo praecipua eius sanctitatis causa, atque idcirco eius gloria, consistit, hoc est: esse nempe aliquid in hominum vita, quod sua dignitate vitam ipsam antecedat; et officium quod ceteris praestet; et spem ita certam, si cum reliquis omnibus comparetur, ut numquam labefactari possit; esse denique in hominibus sanctum quid ac necessarium, cui cetera omnia, ac si res poscat, vita ipsa cedat oportet. Haec autem dignitas, hoc officium, hoc sanctum ac necessarium quid, est religiosae fidei veritas. Atqui haec absoluta fidei praestantia est primum ac maximum elementum in martyris, seu Christi testimonii psychologia: sicut certe primum ac maximum fuit in novensilis Sancti Ioannis Ogilvie, sacerdotis eiusdemque Religiosi professi Societatis Iesu. Homines quidem in martyribus labores atque dolores corporis potissimum considerare consueverunt, id est acerbos cruciatus, quos ipsi passi sunt; causam

**Papal Bull of Canonization of John Ogilvie** 1976
Scottish Catholic Archives

The largest of these emigrations was led by Fr Alexander Macdonell, later Bishop of Kingston, in 1802. By contrast, and possibly better known, is the immigration to Scotland of Irish Catholics in the mid-19th century. Earlier Irish immigrants had tended to integrate well into existing Catholic communities, but after the great famine of the middle of the century, the immigrant population became the larger group and tensions inevitably arose.

The hierarchy of the church was restored in Scotland in 1878, with six dioceses: the Archdiocese of St Andrews and Edinburgh and its suffragan sees of the Dioceses of Aberdeen, Argyll and the Isles, Dunkeld, and Galloway; and the Archdiocese of Glasgow. The second half of the 19th century saw many Religious Orders coming to Scotland under the encouragement of Bishop James Gillis. They assisted the community by providing schools, orphanages and homes for the elderly.

Particularly important in the 20th century was the establishment of two new Dioceses in 1947 – those of Motherwell and Paisley, both in the west, and suffragan sees of the Archdiocese of Glasgow. In 1929 John Ogilvie was beatified, and in 1976 canonized. In June 1935 Scotland had its first Eucharistic Congress, while in 1950 *The Innes Review*, the journal of the Scottish Catholic Historical Association, was founded. By the second half of the 20th century, Catholics were more integrated into, and involved in, Scottish national life to a greater extent than they had ever been since the Reformation. At the same time they were a distinct part of the life of the universal Catholic Church, and in 1982 Scotland enjoyed its first Papal Visit.

# THE NATIONAL LIBRARY OF SCOTLAND: CATULLUS, COLLECTORS & CURATORS

Chris Taylor & Kenneth Dunn,
National Library of Scotland

An Italian secret report on religion, politics and the condition of Catholics in James VI's Scotland; the prayer book of a senior cardinal who was Bonnie Prince Charlie's brother; a medieval Italian manuscript showing that some early Christian scholars thought that the world was round; a Book of Hours belonging to a Tuscan family at the heart of the struggle for control of both the papacy and the Florentine state; a rare book of 1590 by the Pope's civil engineer on raising an ancient obelisk at the centre of St Peter's Square; a beautifully illustrated Book of Hours according to the Use of Rome crafted in Padua; and last but certainly not least, a Renaissance cardinal's manuscript of the poetry of Catullus. The manuscript and printed items in this exhibition are just a few examples of the many treasures of the National Library of Scotland's collections. They demonstrate the influence of Rome on the culture, religion and politics of Scotland.

Since ancient times, Rome has been a source of inspiration as well as a destination for both religious and cultural pilgrimages. Rome has been at the forefront of the development of language, culture, religion, politics and law. Interest in Rome and Roman heritage has therefore held an important place in the collecting of the National Library of Scotland since its foundation in 1925,

Left: **Book of prayers and devotions written for Henry Benedict Stewart, Cardinal Duke of York**, National Library of Scotland

es. unu algore. alt' calore. a quo sol nuq̄ recedit.
Ad illos nuq̄ accedit. alii uo sut hic ardore inde
frigore tpati. Vbi grā. Si ignis i yeme i sbdiuo
accendit'. v. lineas efficere scitur. unā in medio fer
uidā. duas cogelidas. duas i tias tpatas. Quasi
ut sol circuiret in marru v. circulos redderet. Ex
hys circulis. pm septētonal'. scd's solsticial'. Ter
cī equnoctial'. Quartus brumal'. Quit' auptunal'.
noiat'. Sz sol' solsticial' in habitari a nob' nosat'. ha
bitabil' çona q̄ a nob' icollit' i tres partes. medite
rraneo mari diuimit'. Quax una asia. Altera eu
ropa. Tercia affrica dr'. Asia a septentrione p
oriente usq; ad meridie. Europa ab occidente
usq; ad septentrone. Affrica a meridie usq; ad oc
cidente extendit'. Asia a regina eiusde nois e appl
lata. hui' pma regio i orientali parte orbis tiaz
e locus paradisi. longissimo i tiacete spacio. ul'
occeano ul' regionib;. quas no i collit' humanu
gen'. Vnde nec aq̄ diluuij q̄ totā nri orbis sup
ficie altissime coopuerut. Ad eu puenire potue
rut. loc' uidelicet oi amenitate cspicuus. inadi
bil' hoib;. q' igneo muro usq; ad celu est cint'. In
hoc e lignu uite. uidelicet arbor de cui' fructu q
comederit sep in uno statu i mortal' pmanebit.

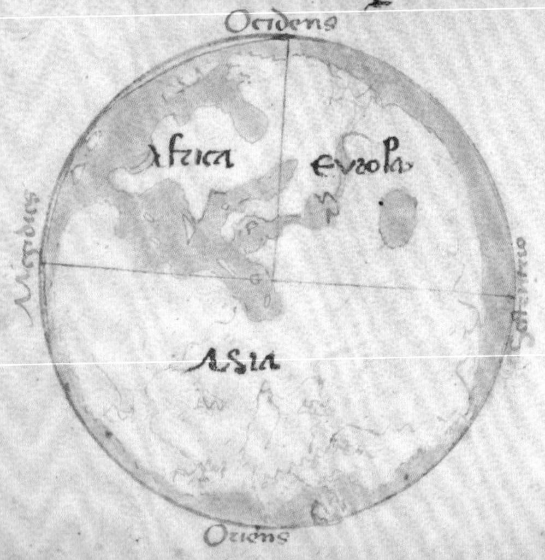

a tradition inherited from its predecessor body, the historic Advocates' Library, which gifted its entire non-legal collections to the nation in that year.

The Library of the Faculty of Advocates was established in the 1680s and its first catalogue demonstrates an early interest in Rome. A fine collection of Latin law books is complemented by histories and works of literature acquired for the continuing education and enjoyment of members of the Faculty and associates. The writings of classical Latin authors include Cicero, Pliny, Tacitus, Virgil, Seneca, Martial and Ovid. Equally the teaching and influence of the Catholic Church is represented by Baptista Platina, Eusebius Pamphili and Pope Pius II. Before he became pope, Pius II had himself been sent to Scotland on a secret diplomatic mission in 1435.

Members of Faculty and their curators assembled a learned library worthy of the ancients as a symbol of their intellectual and cultural status. Like the libraries of Rome, theirs was built on the power and wealth of an empire. Wealth enabled Advocates to travel to Rome and the Italian states which further fuelled interest and passion for the eternal city. Like modern tourists they bought souvenirs which sometimes took the form of manuscripts, books, maps and engravings. Some of these would ultimately find their way into the collections of the Advocates' Library.

An example is provided by Walter Ross, Writer to the Signet, and author of several important legal works. Ross was a keen antiquary, a collector and a patron of the arts. In 1787 he presented the Advocates' Library with a thirteenth century Italian manuscript of Honorius Augustodunensis' *Imago mundi*, based on the 7th century encyclopaedia of the Christian scholar Isidore of Seville. One can imagine the fascination of library patrons as they admired and discussed a medieval manuscript which included two maps showing that an early saint of Rome believed the world was round.

Manuscripts of classical Rome's great authors were keenly pursued by the Library. In the period 1816-1820 the curators acquired Renaissance Cardinal Luigi d'Aragona's copy of Catullus, produced for him by the scribe Ludovicus Regius of Imola. D'Aragona commissioned manuscript copies of classical authors. His manuscript of Catullus probably found a very appreciative new home in the Advocates' Library. Memories of Rome, or anticipation of a visit to Rome, could be kindled by books such as Domenico Fontana's 1590 publication with its superb illustrations of Rome's buildings, together with its explanation of both contemporary and classical techniques.

Left: **Saint Isidore of Seville's 'Mappa Mundi'** National Library of Scotland

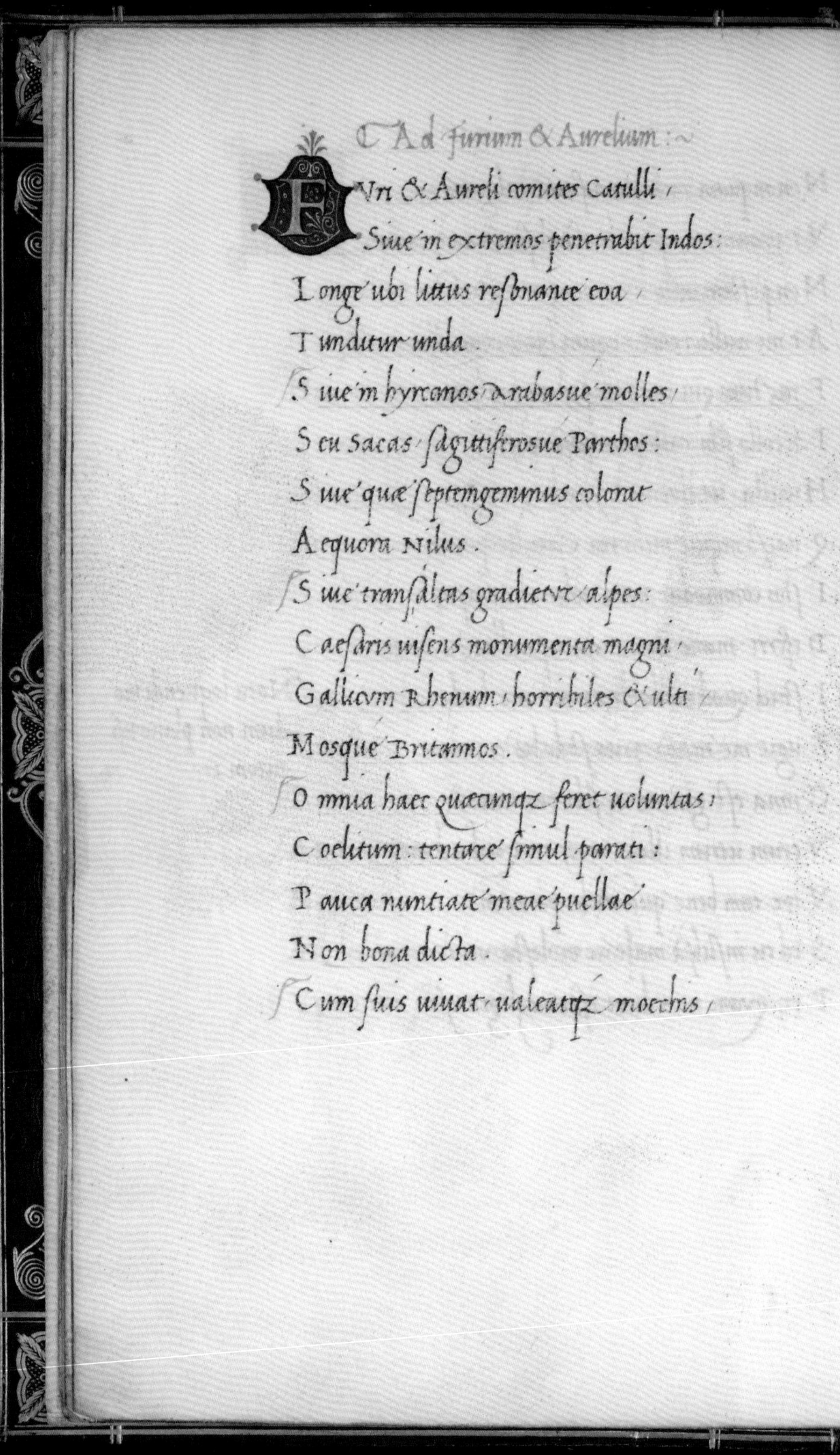

Ad Furium & Aurelium :~

Furi & Aureli comites Catulli,
Siue in extremos penetrabit Indos:
Longe ubi littus resonante eoa
Tunditur unda.
Siue in hyrcanos Arabasue molles,
Seu Sacas sagittiferosue Parthos:
Siue quae septemgeminus colorat
Aequora Nilus.
Siue transaltas gradietur alpes:
Caesaris uisens monumenta magni,
Gallicum Rhenum, horribiles & ulti
Mosque Britannos.
Omnia haec quaecunque feret uoluntas,
Coelitum: tentare simul parati:
Pauca nuntiate meae puellae
Non bona dicta.
Cum suis uiuat ualeatque moechis,

Quos simul complexa tenet trecentos:
Nullum amans uere: sed identidem omnium
Ilia rumpens.
Nec meum respectat ut ante amorem:
Qui illius culpa cecidit, uelut prati
Vltimi flos: praetereunte postquam
Tactus aratro est:~

~: Similitudo :~

Ad Marrucinum Asinium:~

Marrucine asini manu sinistra
Non belle uteris in ioco atque uino:
Tollis lintea negligentiorum.
Hoc falsum esse putas: fugit te inepte:
Quis sordida res & inuenusta est:
Non credis mihi? crede Pollioni
Fratri: qui tua furta uel talento
Mutari uelit: est enim leporum
Disertus puer ac facetiarum.

RELIGIOSAE MAGNIFICENTIAE MONVMENTA
S.$^{MO}$ D.N. SIXTO. V. PONT. OPT. MAX. DIC
DOMENICO FONTANA DA MILI DIOCESE DI COMO ARCHITETTO DI S. SAN. D'ETA D'AN. XLVI
DEL MODO TENVTO NEL TRASPORTARE L'OBELISCO VATICANO. E DELLE FABRICHE FATTE DA NOSTRO SIGNORE SISTO. V. LIBRO. P.$^{O}$
Natalis Bonifacius Sibenicen. Dalmatinus Incidebat. Romae. 1589. Cum Priuilegio Summi Pont.

Sadly, however, during the second half of the 19th century, the Advocates' Library began to run out of space and finds, and was forced to reduce foreign acquisitions. A collection developed around the ideas and spirit of the Renaissance, and the Enlightenment, fell victim to Victorian economic stringency. It is most unfortunate that the Library could not collect books about the 19th century struggle for the control of Rome more comprehensively. A partial redress was achieved by the acquisition of related books by the National Library of Scotland in the next century.

Italian books and manuscripts have been collected by the National Library of Scotland from its beginnings. A very intriguing item was purchased in 1939, a secret Italian report on James VI and Catholicism in Scotland. With Italy and Rome under the control of Mussolini and war looming, there is a little irony in the timing of the purchase and in the report's contents: diplomats are being dispatched; there is much discussion about loyalty, potential switches of allegiance, the role of neutrals; intelligence is being gathered; propaganda is released. It is interesting to reflect that the report's protagonists and subjects had as their recent history the murder Mary Queen of Scots' Italian secretary David Rizzio, Mary's execution, and the threat of the Spanish Armada as a potential agency for the restoration of

**Book of Hours according to the Use of Rome,** Florence, c.1450-60, National Library of Scotland

**Book of Hours according to the Use of Rome,** probably Padua, late 15th century, National Library of Scotland

Left: **Domenico Fontana, *Della transportatione dell'obelisco vaticano...*** Rome, 1590, National Library of Scotland

The National Library of Scotland's new building on George IV Bridge was completed and officially opened in 1956. Curators collected European books under the direction of the Librarian, Professor William Beattie, who oversaw the purchase of John Purves's fine collection of Italian books. Purves was the founder of the Italian Department at Edinburgh University: he had an interest in Italian manuscripts of all periods, and in the city of Florence. This collecting tradition was endorsed by the Library's purchase at Sotheby's in 1960 of the two Books of Hours shown in the exhibition.

The Library continues to develop its Italian collections which help inform the research interests of students and scholars of history, art history, literature and language. New interests have developed too. Library readers research the influence of Italian Christian Democrat factions and the attempt at the historic compromise with the Left. The ancient humour of Catullus has been joined in the reading rooms by more modern writers who have discussed the politics and influence of Rome such as Alberto Moravia, Carlo Levi, Leonardo Sciascia, Umberto Eco and Giancarlo De Cataldo. Perhaps the founding fathers of the Advocates' Library would have taken a special interest in the writing of their fellow professional who is now a successful author, Giancarlo De Cataldo.

**Domenico Fontana, *Della transportatione dell'obelisco vaticano...*** Rome, 1590, National Library of Scotland

18
H
B
B
A
E
E
E

Gavin Hamilton, ***Douglas Hamilton, 8th Duke of Hamilton, with Dr John Moore and Ensign John Moore*** c.1775-77
Scottish National Portrait Gallery

# ITALY & THE SCOTS IN THE AGE OF THE GRAND TOUR

Dr Patricia Andrew

The Grand Tour was a phenomenon particularly associated with younger members of the British aristocracy and gentry of the 18th century. The custom had started earlier, the name 'Grand Tour' being coined by Richard Lassels in his book *The Voyage of Italy* of 1670. It was at its height from the 1740s to the 1790s; became suppressed during the wars with France; and subsequently enjoyed a brief revival in the 1820s before the age of mass travel arrived in the mid-19th century.

The British were by no means the only nationality to make the Grand Tour, but they were the most numerous participants, and largely set the tone and pattern for other northern European countries. They travelled on the Continent for up to three or four years, enjoying what was supposed to be a period of education, cultural improvement, the acquisition of manners, polish and sophisticated taste – though for many it was more an extended 'gap year', entailing the expenditure of vast quantities of parental funds, and the liberal sowing of wild oats. It was something of a rite of passage, and included the purchasing and commissioning of paintings, sculpture and books to enhance the family seat. Many Scottish families collected over several generations of Grand Tours, for example the Hopes of Hopetoun and the Clerks of Penicuik.

The Grand Tour took in many European cities, but the focus was always Italy, and the primary goal always Rome. The British generally stayed in the area around Piazza di Spagna, a quarter known as the Ghetto degli Inglesi. They spent very freely, employing servants and guides or *ciceroni*, renting apartments, purchasing antique sculpture and Old Master paintings, and the fashionable clothes and accessories of the day. This led to a huge industry and a large, long-term British community.

The Scots had to be content with being described as *Inglesi*, though this referred to their language rather than their nationality. The Italian term used for Grand Tourists came from the French address for a young British gentleman – *Milord* – so they were referred to collectively as the *Milordi*.

**David Allan, *A Roman Coffee House*** c.1775
National Gallery of Scotland

These young men went furnished with an education that included far more knowledge of the classical world than of the contemporary one. Even the laziest knew their Virgil and Horace, and the map of ancient Latium. James Boswell, rather better read than most, was so excited and overwhelmed after being guided around Rome by Scotsman Colin Morison that he wrote 'I was seized with enthusiasm. I began to speak Latin'. But modern Rome was equally inspiring, with its huge and magnificent architecture, and its festivals and spectacles such as the elaborate annual public firework display, the Girandola, at Castel Sant'Angelo.

All this travelling, studying, and purchasing of antiquities by young and inexperienced Grand Tourists required an army of guides, antiquaries, agents and dealers, some of them eminent early archaeologists and *cognoscenti*. Generally termed antiquarians, many were very erudite, one of the foremost being James

Byres (1734–1817), a serious Etruscan scholar. Born in Aberdeenshire of a Jacobite family, he had left Scotland after 1745, had been educated in France, and worked in Italy from 1758 to 1790, contributing significantly to the formation of neo-classical taste in Britain.

There were also numerous artists, architects and antiquaries who came for a period of study, but who often stayed for many years and in some cases never returned to Britain. They had no difficulty finding careers as copyists of Old Master paintings in addition to working on their own compositions, and they also acted as restorers (or fakers) and dealers.

Rome was also the home of the Jacobites, the exiled Stewart claimants to the British throne. Until 1766 the Stewart court had an official status in Rome, enjoying papal protection and representation at the Vatican. There was, however, a considerable diplomatic ambivalence, as successive popes gave personal audiences to important Protestant Grand Tourists, and many Protestant visitors were happy to hire Catholic guides and dealers. The visitors were always keen to glimpse the Jacobite court in Rome, the members and adherents of which became in a sense one of the sights of the city. There was also the delicious whiff of intrigue surrounding possible spies such as the egregious Abbé Peter Grant (1708-1784), a Gaelic-speaking priest who was such a staunch supporter and friend to many a struggling British artist.

Rome held a cultural importance for the British beyond its physical boundaries. Its local landscape and archaeology were well known to northerners, an idealised concept through classical writing which had been enhanced by the more recent visual images created by the classical landscape painters of the 17th century. The most 'perfect' example, and the one most quoted in literature and visual images, was Tivoli, some twenty kilometres from Rome. 'Tivoli temples' sprung up all over Britain, and one example is St Bernard's Well on the Water of Leith in Edinburgh, commissioned by Lord Gardenstone, who visited Italy in the 1780s.

IACOBVS·III·D·G·ANG·SCOT·FRANC ET HIBER·REX

# THE NATIONAL GALLERIES OF SCOTLAND: SCOTTISH PERCEPTIONS OF ROME

Dr Patricia Andrew

The National Galleries of Scotland hold an outstanding collection of Italian art, from the medieval period to the modern day. Most of the items selected for this exhibition, however, reflect the theme of travel to Rome in the age of the Grand Tour, by diplomats, exiled royalty, artists, antiquaries, and by the Grand Tourists themselves.

The first item is from the 17th century, before the Grand Tour proper began, and forms a cultural link with items loaned to the exhibition by the National Library of Scotland: a book by an artist, John Michael Wright, who was first in Rome in the 1640s. He returned in 1686 to document the embassy sent to the Vatican under Roger Palmer, the Earl of Castlemaine (1634-1705), by King James VII and II. Lord Castlemaine's procession to his formal audience of the Pope comprised over 300 coaches. The splendour and magnificence of the occasion is recorded in Wright's book, published first in Italian in 1687, then in an expanded English edition in 1688.

By this time, the formalised tradition of the Grand Tour had begun, and the institution had acquired its name. Antiquarians such as Gavin Hamilton

Left: **John Michael Wright, *An Account of His Excellence Roger, Earl of Castlemaine's Embassy London*** 1688 National Gallery of Scotland

(1723 - 1798), who spent most of his career in Rome, were influential in the dissemination of the neo-classical style, and his series of grand history paintings was much admired. Hamilton painted comparatively few portraits, but one notable exception shows a young Grand Tourist, the 8th Duke of Hamilton, with his tutor Dr John Moore (and his son, the future military hero Sir John Moore 'of Corunna'), who gesture in vain towards the antiquities of the city. The Duke, alas, showed little interest in them, but rather more in girls, clothes and horses.

A more everyday life for Scots in Rome is depicted in David Allan's watercolour image of a Roman coffee house. These establishments were hubs of social life for artists and students, and this example may show the celebrated English Coffee House, which also acted as the British *poste restante* ('English' denotes English-language, and thus British). Allan's many informal figure and character drawings have an immediacy sometimes lacking in more formal oil paintings of the Roman scene, and he depicted many street scenes with local inhabitants and tradespeople in traditional costume. He also made a drawing of Henry Benedict, Cardinal York (younger brother of 'Bonnie Prince Charlie') at morning prayer. The drawing is a great contrast to the colourful, commemorative oil painting produced some fifty years earlier by Agostino Masucci (1691-1758) to commemorate the Solemnisation of the Marriage of Prince James Francis Edward Stewart (the 'Old Pretender') and Princess Maria Clementina Sobieska, at Montefiascone in 1719.

Allan Ramsay (1713-1784), named after his poet father and Edinburgh character – whose statue stands near the Royal Scottish Academy building – became internationally renowned for his outstanding portraits. He was unique in making four visits to Italy in the course of his long career, two mainly for artistic study and two for antiquarian research. His watercolour of the interior of the Colosseum was made in 1755, probably on a sketching trip with the Scottish architect Robert Adam and the French artist and draughtsman Charles-Louis Clérisseau.

A less well-known student of architecture, preparing for a professional career in Scotland, was the Edinburgh architect and mason, John Baxter (c.1740-1798). His drawings include one of a column capital in the Villa Colonna. This delicate study in black chalk, with a measuring scale on the left-hand margin, is typical of

pp.38-9: **Agostino Masucci, *Solemnisation of the Marriage of Prince James Francis Edward Stewart and Princess Maria Clementina Sobieska, Montefiascone, 1719*** c.1735, National Gallery of Scotland

Left: **John Brown, *The Basilica of Maxentius and Constantine, Rome*** 1774-76 (detail) National Gallery of Scotland

the contemporary interest in architectural ornament and shows familiarity with the work of James Adam, himself a notable Roman visitor of the 1760s.

Most of the Scottish artists who studied in Italy returned home, but a few remained for the rest of their lives. Jacob More (1740-93), from Edinburgh, was one of these. He worked as a landscape painter, garden-designer and dealer, and became such a central figure in the artistic community that he earned the sobriquet 'More of Rome'. His friend and executor Richard Cooper (c.1740-c.1820), who had spent some years in Italy in the 1770s, made an elegiac drawing in 1801 of More's tomb in the Protestant Cemetery, beside the ancient wall and in the shadow of the Pyramid of Cestius.

Above: **Richard Cooper, *The Pyramid of Caius Cestius and the Tomb of Jacob More*** 1801
National Gallery of Scotland

Facing page left: **Allan Ramsay, *The Interior of the Colosseum*** 1755
National Gallery of Scotland

**Geoff Uglow (b.1979),** ***Sempre Lo Stesso*** 2006
Lent by the artist

# THE ROYAL SCOTTISH ACADEMY & ITALY: CONTEMPORARY ENLIGHTENMENT

Colin R. Greenslade, Royal Scottish Academy

The patronage of art is age-old. The funding of creativity by benefactors has shaped the art world as we know it. It could be argued that this is observed most of all in the magnificent cities of Italy – Rome, Venice and Florence. Historical cities of commerce and patronage; of learning, exploration and vision; and of wealth and grandeur. Cities that can boast some of the most beautiful art and architecture in existence.

Artists and architects still need patronage today, a requirement which the Royal Scottish Academy encourages and supports through its programme of awards and scholarships. For nearly forty years, the Academy, through its administration of the John Kinross scholarships, has enabled emerging artists and architects to visit Italy, and Florence in particular, to explore and to be inspired. Funding their travel and accommodation and, most importantly, their time, the Kinross Scholarships allow graduates to absorb the influences of the Italian experience, one that has proved to be an invaluable opportunity as they make the transition from university study to careers.

Italy, of course, has been an inspiration to generations of artists and travellers. And in recognition of the tradition of the Grand Tour of over two centuries

**Steven MacIver** (b.1978), ***San Pietro*** 2006 **(not on display)**, Photograph courtesy of the British School at Rome

ago, our scholars find much to excite, bewilder and enthral them, before they return to Scotland to show us the results of their endeavours. For these scholars, eager in their quests of discovery, learning and development, the experience of widened horizons is committed to paper, canvas and film. Their interpretations of what they have viewed and recorded give us an insight into the wealth of their Italian experience, translating the information into new artworks and designs for buildings. Like the Grand Tourists, it is a passing-on of influence and experience.

Both Geoff Uglow and Steven MacIver, exhibiting here in *Scotland and Rome*, were beneficiaries of the John Kinross Scholarship. Both artists employed their time in Italy to develop the direction of their subsequent careers: Geoff, with his interest in re-visiting history and antiquity; and Steven, with his interest in public arenas, meeting places and stadia. Both artists were subsequently awarded the Sainsbury Scholarship to the British School at Rome, which enabled them to live and work in the city for an extended period, and further develop their careers as artists. Coincidentally, both artists met in Rome as their scholarships overlapped – interesting that they should have taken similar paths to get there, and are still connected through friendship, and RSA activities.

**Steven MacIver** (b.1978), ***Sant' Agnese*** 2006, Lent by the artist

When the family of John Kinross, RSA, initiated the award for new graduates to visit and explore Italy, they would no doubt have had some vision of the impact the scholarship might have on Scotland's artists and architects, but probably not of the significance that their legacy has meant to so many.

In addition, the relationship which the Royal Scottish Academy has developed with the Italian Cultural Institute in Edinburgh has also paved the way for many scholars. The Institute has been instrumental in the development of initiatives that provide a wider agenda for Kinross Scholars in Italy, for example, by awarding museum passes to Scholars for free entry to museums. The RSA looks forward to a further strengthening of this bond with the Institute, with a view to developing opportunities and platforms for artists of both countries. Indeed, we hope that this relationship might enable the development of a larger collaborative infrastructure between Scotland and Italy for artists and architects of both nationalities to experience new directions and create new possibilities...

# THE ITALIAN COMMUNITY IN SCOTLAND TODAY

Gabriele Papadia de Bottini,
Consul General of Italy in Scotland & Northern Ireland

Throughout the centuries, countless connections have linked Italy with this part of the United Kingdom, and the relationship has continued into the 20th and 21st centuries in various new forms. The Italian community which settled in Scotland at the beginning of last century had a strong and marked identity, originating mainly from the Province of Frosinone, south-east of Rome, and from the Garfagnana area in Tuscany.

These people, often from an underprivileged background, thanks to their hard work – initially mainly in the catering trade – have not only succeeded in achieving full integration, but have also been able to build for themselves and their families a substantial level of prosperity, achieving, in some cases, eminent positions in the economic, political and cultural fields of their adopted country, while never relinquishing the bond with their homeland.

The Second World War was a sorrowful chapter for Italians resident in the UK. The sinking of the SS Arandora Star in July 1940, in which 447 Italian interned civilians died, has deeply marked the Community: the memorial monument which is being built on the occasion of the 70th anniversary of the tragedy, in the new cloister of Glasgow's Roman Catholic Cathedral, will also symbolise a

Members of the Italian Community in Scotland at the end of a charity bike ride from Edinburgh to Picinisco (near Rome)
photo by Mario Alonzi

moment of remembrance and reconciliation. In the same way, the Italian Chapel, built by the Italian prisoners of war in Orkney, is considered one of the most significant and touching Scottish monuments.

Today there are approximately 11,000 Italian nationals registered with the Consulate General in Edinburgh, although it is estimated that around 30,000 Italians are currently in Scotland, and roughly 50,000 people resident in Scotland are of Italian origin (about 1% of the total population).

From a social viewpoint, in the last twenty years the composition of our Community in Scotland has been characterised by new trends: beside the traditional occupations, a new generation of Italian academics, businessmen, medical doctors and scientists have been increasingly attracted by Scotland's dynamic entrepreneurial, scientific and academic framework. In such a promising context the Italian Consulate General and the Cultural Institute, together with their Scottish counterparts, continue to support and promote various initiatives in the institutional, economic and cultural sectors, aimed at strengthening and developing bilateral relations.

De saint george martir. Antienne.

Fideles hic attendite. xp̄i sanctum diligite mentibus letis dicite. georgi martyr inclite. te decet laus et gloria. predotatum milicia. per quem puella regia. existens ĩ tristicia. coram dracone pessimo. se reddidit altissimo.

# ROME & SCOTLAND: A BACKGROUND FOR THE VISITOR

Dr Raymond McCluskey, University of Glasgow

Alert visitors to Rome, passing through Piazza Barberini and beginning to make the sedate climb along the Via delle Quattro Fontane, will perhaps be astonished to find the British royal coat of arms high above an otherwise unornamented doorway. He or she will have stumbled upon the former site of the Pontifical Scots College which, for centuries before its removal in the 1960s to the Via Cassia in the outskirts of the city, was the home of generations of Scots training for the Catholic priesthood. For those who lived there and visited over the decades, this was a little piece of Scotland at the heart of the Eternal City. Our visitors, briskly continuing on for a mere five minutes and turning a corner into Via XX Settembre, might now alight upon a building in the Florentine palazzo style so beloved of the 19th century. Set back some distance from the pavement, the nameplate at the gate identifies the building as St Andrew's Presbyterian Church. In sympathy with the complexities of history, this outpost of the Church of Scotland dates from a time when the winds of change unleashed by the forces of the mid-century movement for Italian unification (*Risorgimento*) made it possible for a church of the Reformed tradition to open its doors in Rome in the 1880s – but only in a building which did not publicly identify its ecclesiastical purpose.

Left: **Hours of Marie de Rieux** 15th century
Scottish Catholic Archives

The Pontifical Scots College. St. Andrew's Presbyterian Church. These are but two representatives in the city itself of the colourful relationship between Rome and Scotland which extends over more than two millennia. But Rome has been more than a physical place to Scots. While many Scots, over the ages, may not have had the opportunity to visit the city itself, Rome has, in so many ways, visited them and shaped the world in which they have lived. Rome is an idea which has inhabited the mind: a source of law; a font of spirituality; a wellspring of inspiration in the arts, architecture, literature, and music; a goal of pilgrimage prompted by intellectual curiosity as well as religious feelings. At the same time, Rome has continued to throw up its contradictions for Scots. As a consequence of the Protestant Reformation of the 16th century, Rome became, for a great many Scots, synonymous with obscurantism. With the coming of the 18th-century Enlightenment, however, and the beginnings of the traditions of the Grand Tour, well-heeled Scots would once again revel in the delights of the city, celebrating the relics of its classical past while treating its religion with benevolent, if at times patronising, civility. In modern times, countless others have made the journey by land, sea, and air. In the context of the 'global village' in which we all now live, Scotland and Rome have never been closer.

Let us now look a little more closely at several key themes in the history of the relationship between Scotland and Rome.

## *Ancient and Classical Rome in Scotland*

The fabled cry of the Scots – 'Wha' daur meddle wi' me?' (Who dares meddle with me?) which has become so much part of an identity marked by a strong streak of independence – may owe its origins in the popular imaginations of 21st-century Scots and not, as one might expect, to tales of 'Braveheart', Robert Bruce and the Battle of Bannockburn (1314), but to the distant memory of an even earlier era.

When the Romans first invaded Caledonia (their name for Scotland) in AD 71, they probably did so as a proactive response to what was perceived as the threat of foraging tribes of Votadini and Selgovae across the most north-westerly border of the Empire. For later generations of Scots, however, the perception that the mighty Romans were unable to conquer their Caledonian ancestors provided the foundations for a myth of Pictish and Celtic invincibility. However, the Romans did leave their mark on the contours of the north British landscape with, most notably, Hadrian's Wall, and its successor, the Antonine Wall. Other less imposing sites are scattered across the land, uncovered by the careful efforts of archaeologists over the decades. Some, like the Bearsden Baths (in the environs of Glasgow), are the fortunate result of a builder's excavations in advance of modern development. Indeed, the fruits of chance finds of artefacts such as burial stones, coins, statuary and jewellery are to be found in many local museums in Scotland and provide clues to the social and cultural histories of their age. But, while much can be discovered with some certainty about life in Scotland during this period, sometimes, frustratingly, the history of even key events is decidedly vague. Most famously, the Roman historian Tacitus (56-117) provides an account of the great Battle of Mons Graupius (in 83 or 84) at which the Roman army defeated a tribal alliance. To this day, historians cannot agree on the location where the battle took place: the archaeological legacy of the various disputed sites (generally in the north-east of the country) is insufficient to be conclusive, and must remain, for the present, a matter of scholarly speculation.

**Bronze anchor-shaped brooch**
Hunterian Museum, University of Glasgow

## *Medieval Scotland*

The presence of a cross, probably of the 7th century, in the museum in Whithorn (Galloway), its truncated inscription naming St Peter, serves as a solitary witness from Scotland's early centuries of a link with the Roman cult of the apostle who by tradition was martyred in Rome. In later centuries, a much more physically imposing link with European Christianity was to be found in the great monasteries, of which Jedburgh, Kelso, and Melrose, founded in the reign of King David I (reigned 1124-53), are the most famous. Though Rome itself could not claim to be the seat of origin of the orders from which these communities sprang – other localities such as Cluny and Cîteaux in France might rightly make stronger claims – there is still no doubt that the patronage of monastic life in Scotland during the 12th and 13th centuries was a reflection of a conscious choice by powerful men and influential women to be seen to sponsor the 'latest approved model' in an era when a reforming papacy aimed to promote a sense of religious and social cohesion throughout the West. Contemporary chroniclers underlined this image of the 'seamless robe' through reference to 'Christendom' rather than 'Europe' – and the monasteries in Scotland were like braiding on the 'robe'. They represented not only the power and influence of their patrons, but also a sense of communion with others of their order (Benedictines, Cistercians, etc) and with the Church in general. Liturgical prayers for the Pope and for the monarch best sum up the way in which the religious life of the Middle Ages managed to maintain and negotiate the tension between the 'local' Church (and its political masters on the doorstep, as it were) and its allegiance to the Apostolic See of Rome.

In fact, the link with Rome was to feature large in defining Scottish nationhood. Scottish bishops were keen to preserve their independence from the claims of the Archbishops of York to be their superiors. Kings, as well as churchmen, petitioned Rome throughout the later medieval centuries in a series of diplomatic initiatives designed to achieve papal approval of Scottish claims. Pope Alexander III (reigned 1159-81) bolstered Scottish ambitions with his declaration that Glasgow was a 'special daughter of the Roman Church', a title extended to all other Scottish dioceses (except Whithorn) by Pope Celestine III (reigned 1191-98) in 1192. Later still, the Scottish Church's independence from English authority was further underlined with the promotion of both St Andrews (1472) and Glasgow (1492) to the status of Archdioceses. The history of Scotland's evolving nationhood is, clearly, inseparable from the story of its links with Rome. Most famous of all examples, perhaps, the Declaration of Arbroath of 1320, in which the nobles and magnates of Scotland declared their independence from the English crown, was addressed to Pope John XXII (reigned 1316-34, though not actually resident in Rome). The reverence with which this particular testament to liberty is held may have become stronger among later generations, which have chosen, anachronistically, to endow the document with democratic and self-determining aspirations. But, nevertheless, it needs to be acknowledged that, in the face of English aggrandisement, it was to the papacy that the Scottish kingdom turned for legitimisation of its continuing assertions of independence. This was simply the 'way of the world' in those days. In appealing to the pope, the Scottish Crown and nobility were no different from other potentates of Europe who experienced similar incursions into their lands.

## *Renaissance and Baroque*

Between 1309 and 1378, circumstances took the popes from Rome to Avignon where an impressive pontifical palace still overawes. Given its huge dimensions, the Avignon residence hardly gives the impression that it was intended to have been temporary. But the papacy did return to Rome in 1378, only to be caught up in a Schism which, at one stage in the early 15th century, saw rival popes in Rome, Avignon and Florence. Perhaps reflecting the tradition of 'Auld Alliance' with the French, Scotland sided with the Avignon papacy and, indeed, in 1383, Clement VII created the bishop of Glasgow, Walter Wardlaw, a cardinal. (Because Clement VII is now identified in official papal lists as an antipope, Wardlaw's claim to be the first Scottish cardinal is somewhat more dubious that it otherwise would have been.)

By the time the papacy had returned to Rome permanently, in the 15th century, the spirit of the Renaissance was already flowering. Traditionally, the origins of the Renaissance are associated with Florence, but Rome was not slow in providing opportunities for artistic geniuses to contribute to the creation and decoration of a new city which would replace the faded structures of the Middle Ages. Scholars, too, would be encouraged to broaden their understanding and imitation of the classical world, for example through the search for accurate texts and the removal of the accretions of erroneous manuscript copies over centuries. This was the world of Lorenzo Valla (1406-57), a great Renaissance humanist scholar, as much as Michelangelo (1475-1564) or Raphael (1483-1520).

The influence of the Renaissance in Scotland was particularly visible under the patronage of James IV (reigned 1488-1513). It can now be seen in the architecture of Falkland Palace in Fife, and in the scholarship of both Hector Boece (1465-1536), first Principal of Aberdeen University and an acquaintance of Erasmus of Rotterdam, and of John Mair (1467-1550) at the University of St Andrews. Indeed, the establishment of both Glasgow and Aberdeen Universities by papal bulls in 1451 (Pope Nicholas V) and 1495 (Pope Alexander VI) respectively is a sign of the continuing links between Rome and Scotland, and of a desire to allow Scots to share in the new learning of the age under the auspices of the Apostolic See. Glasgow looked in particular to the University of Bologna as its model, with its strong reputation for the study of Roman Law; the importance attached to this body of law in Scotland helps, in part, to explain the significant differences in the legal inheritances and customs of Scotland and England (a distictiveness noted and protected in the Treaty of Union in 1707). The Protestant Reformation of the second half of the 16th century clearly transformed the relationship between Scotland and Rome, perhaps most colourfully exemplified in the turbulent life of the Catholic Mary, Queen of Scots (1542-87). Yet, despite a growing emphasis on the vernacular in worship, Protestant scholars such as George Buchanan (1506-

Baxter Rome
71

82), tutor to James VI, still inhabited an intellectual landscape dominated by the language bequeathed by Rome, namely Latin.

The baroque period, covering most of the 17th and part of the 18th centuries, has different connotations in Roman and Scottish contexts. While Catholic Europe embraced the models of church architecture and decoration which dominated the period – altarpieces filled with cherubs and other exuberances, for example – the reformed tradition of the Scottish Church offered a more sober environment for worship. The description 'baroque', however, encompasses more than the physical arts of buildings. It denotes, too, a period in music represented by composers such as Arcangelo Corelli (1653-1713) in Rome: Sir John Clerk of Penicuik (1676-1755) is one Scot who studied under him during his stay in the city.

## *Impact of the Grand Tour: Neo-classicism and Romanticism*

With the zenith of the Grand Tour in the 18th century, a renewed vigour in the imaginative and inspirational relationship between Rome and Scotland can be seen. The Tour was a journey of discovery and education through France, central Europe and Italy, undertaken by many young men of independent means. During the course of their travels, artists and authors had opportunities to explore the heritage of Rome at first hand. In the realm of the arts, Robert Adam (1728-92) and Allan Ramsay (1713-84) were among the most notable Scots to have spent formative periods in Rome. The painter Gavin Hamilton (1723-98) settled in the city for most of his life, working as a painter of classical scenes and as an archaeologist; he also painted a representation of the martyrdom of St Andrew as an altarpiece for Sant'Andrea degli Scozzesi, the church of the Pontifical Scots College. Hamilton's paintings capture the essence of the neo-classical style, and promoted it. His profile-portrait of the poet William Hamilton of Bangour (1704-54) would not have looked out of place as a mural on the wall of an ancient Roman villa; his *Oath of Brutus* depicts figures reminiscent of classical sculpture. The most popular portraitist in Rome, Pompeo Batoni (1708-87), was on one occasion requested by a Scottish sitter to portray him with a curious mix of Scottish and Roman symbols: Colonel the Hon. William Gordon of Fyvie (1736-1816) was depicted in 1766 with a tartan plaid swept around his body in the style of a toga, with the ruins of the Colosseum in the background. This was one of many portraits by Batoni made for the visiting aristocracy and gentry, to be transported home as flattering souvenirs to Scotland.

Left: **John Baxter, *Column capital in the Villa Colonna*** 1765
National Gallery of Scotland

CHORVS
Da. Allan del^t 1773

## *Jacobites and Rome*

The Jacobite rebellions of the first half of the 18th century stimulated the Scottish Romantic imagination in the 19th century. John Blake Macdonald's painting (1863) of *Charles Edward Stewart Taking his Leave of Scotland*, and Robert Louis Stevenson's novel *Kidnapped* (1886), are representative of the age. While it is erroneous to believe that the Jacobites who supported the causes of the deposed James II and VII (1633-1701), his son James (1688-1766, the Old Pretender, begetter of the 1715 Rebellion) and his grandson Charles Edward (1720-88, the Young Pretender, leader of the 1745 Rebellion) were uniformly Catholic – many, in fact, were Episcopalians – Rome was nevertheless a principal theatre for Jacobite machinations and many Scottish exiles were known to visit the alternative royal court in the Palazzo del Re. Amongst other assumed roles, such exiles acted as guides for visitors to local sites, offering advice, for example, on antiquarian purchases. However, fortunes for the exiles began to change with the death of James 'III' as the pope refused to recognise Charles Edward as king – an indication of a new *realpolitik* of rapprochement with the House of Hanover. Jacobite patronage in Rome was vital for many Scottish exiles: visitors and artists such as Katharine Read (1723-78) and Ann Forbes (1745-1834) benefitted from the ready connections which the Jacobite network provided. The decline of Charles Edward – the sometime 'Bonnie Prince' – is tragic indeed. Charles died in Rome, his claim to the British throne all but ignored by the Roman authorities (who were none too pleased when the Pontifical Scots College continued for a period to refer to Charles Edward in the style of a king despite papal prohibition). Charles Edward's brother, Henry Benedict (1725-1807), Cardinal York, then promoted himself as Henry IX, but the gesture rang hollow in a Europe whose politics had now passed the Jacobite cause by. But culturally, as part of the fabric of Scottish history, the Jacobite story survives in its constant retelling in everything from picture books for children to serious academic studies. Rome is inextricably linked with this story. Indeed, there is a certain irony in the fact that one of the most beautiful monuments in St Peter's basilica is the memorial to the Stewarts, by Antonio Canova (1757-1822). Many is the Scottish visitor who has taken time to look more closely at this reminder of the vicissitudes of the history of their native country, found under the soaring roof of the mighty basilica.

Left: **David Allan, *Cardinal York at Morning Prayer*** 1773
National Gallery of Scotland

## *The Victorian Period*

As the 19th century progressed, neo-classicism gradually gave way to a new approach to artists' work which found expression in the Romantic movement. One of the developing characteristics of this period is its fascination with the medieval world, rather than the classical – but Rome still remained an inspiration, fuelling some ambitious architectural projects. The world was changing rapidly with the advent of the railways, and the remarkable proliferation of new discoveries and inventions in the wake of increasing industrialisation and urbanisation. Robert Macpherson (1814-72) left Scotland for Rome where initially he set himself up as an artist, but eventually achieved greater fame in the city as a master of the new art of photography. Macpherson's life truly encapsulates the social and cultural transformations of his age and his photographs provide some of the first glimpses of Rome in the reign of Pope Pius IX (reigned 1846-78). Yet, while we might today consider the photograph better able to represent a reality which painting cannot capture, this is, in fact, a misunderstanding of both crafts and was certainly not the dominant perception in Macpherson's day. Indeed, images of Rome, photographed, sketched or painted, continued to feed imaginations beyond those of poets and artists. The fate of Rome during the process of Italian unification in the 1860s was an issue which frequently featured in the foreign intelligence columns of Scottish newspapers. Some Scots went so far as to join Garibaldi's army; others (mainly of Irish origin) joined the papal army in defence of Rome. Ironically, it was in the aftermath of the fall of Rome in 1870, and the imposed status of the pope as the 'Prisoner of the Vatican', that well-to-do Scottish Catholic pilgrims took advantage of improving rail links and the services of Thomas Cook's travel advisers to visit Rome on several occasions for papal jubilees.

Right: **Robert Macpherson**
***Via de Sugherari, the Theatre of Marcellus, Rome*** c.1860
Albumen Print
Scottish National Portrait Gallery

VIA DE
SUGHERARI
30
31

# LIST OF EXHIBITS

## University of Glasgow

***Monumenta Romani Imperii...***
Glasgow, 1768
Glasgow University Library, Special Collections Department
(Sp. Coll. Hunterian H.2.20)

**Altar to Fortuna**
Hunterian Museum: F.21

**Head of a Goddess**
Hunterian Museum: F.1993.1

**Fountainhead**
Hunterian Museum: 138045

**Statuette of Fortuna**
Hunterian Museum: F.43

**Bronze Head of Minerva**
Hunterian Museum: F.1990.18

**Sadlerhead Jug**
Hunterian Museum: F.55

**Bronze Satyr Head**
Hunterian Museum: 138052

**Child's Leather Shoe** (*carbatina*)
Hunterian Museum: F.1936.121

**Bronze Double-chain Brooch**
Hunterian Museum: A.1980.2

**Bronze Anchor-shaped Brooch**
Hunterian Museum: A.1980.1

**A Group of 18 Roman Coins**
Hunterian Museum

## Scottish Catholic Archives

**Papal Bull for founding the Scots Benedictine Abbey of St James, Ratisbon** 1177
SK/1/1

**Arma Christi** 15th century
CB/57/9

**Hours of Marie de Rieux** 15th century
CB/57/2

**Letter of Mary, Queen of Scots to Archbishop Beaton** 1571
JB/2/2/5

**Papal Bull of Canonization of John Ogilvie** 1976
JO/4

**Account of reception of Prince Charles Edward Stewart at Pontifical Scots College, Rome** 1765
CA/3/15/16

## National Library of Scotland

**Domenico Fontana, *Della transportatione dell'obelisco vaticano...***
Rome, 1590
Al.1.31

**Manuscript of poems of Catallus copied by the scribe Ludovicus Regius of Imola** 1495
Adv. MS.18.5.2

**Book of prayers and devotions written for Henry Benedict Stewart, Cardinal York**
MS.21238